Terrorism &
Perceived Terrorism Threats

Bully on Campus & Online

Drugs & Alcohol

Gunman on Campus

Natural Disasters

Navigating Cyberspace

Peer Pressure & Relationships

Protecting Your Body: Germs, Superbugs, Poison, & Deadly Diseases

Road Safety

Sports

Stranger Danger

Terrorism & Perceived Terrorism Threats

Terrorism &
Perceived Terrorism Threats

Christie Marlowe

Mason Crest

Mason Crest
450 Parkway Drive, Suite D
Broomall, PA 19008
www.masoncrest.com

Printed and bound in the United States of America.

First printing
9 8 7 6 5 4 3 2 1

Series ISBN: 978-1-4222-3044-2
ISBN: 978-1-4222-3055-8
ebook ISBN: 978-1-4222-8839-9

Library of Congress Cataloging-in-Publication Data

Marlowe, Christie.
  Terrorism & perceived terrorism threats / Christie Marlowe.
      pages cm. – (Safety first)
  Includes index.
  Audience: Ages 10+
  Audience: Grade 4 to 6.
  ISBN 978-1-4222-3055-8 (hardback)—ISBN 978-1-4222-3044-2 (series)—ISBN 978-1-4222-8839-9 (ebook) 1. Terrorism–Juvenile literature. 2. Terrorism–Prevention–Juvenile literature. I. Title.
  HV6431.M36467 2015
  363.325–dc23
                                2014003856

Contents

Introduction

No task is more important than creating safe schools for all children. It should not require an act of courage for parents to send their children to school nor for children to come to school. As adults, we must do everything reasonable to provide a school climate that is safe, secure, and welcoming—an environment where learning can flourish. The educational effectiveness and the strength of any nation is dependent upon a strong and effective educational system that empowers and prepares young people for meaningful and purposeful lives that will promote economic competitiveness, national defense, and quality of life.

Clearly adults are charged with the vital responsibility of creating a positive educational climate. However, the success of young people is also affected by their own participation. The purpose of this series of books is to articulate what young adults can do to ensure their own safety, while at the same time educating them as to the steps that educators, parents, and communities are taking to create and maintain safe schools. Each book in the series gives young people tools that will empower them as participants in this process. The result is a model where students have the information they need to work alongside parents, educators, and community leaders to tackle the safety challenges that face young people every day.

Perhaps one of the most enduring and yet underrated challenges facing young adults is bullying. Ask parents if they can remember the schoolyard bully from when they were in school, and the answers are quite revealing. Unfortunately, the situation is no better today—and new venues for bullying exist in the twenty-first-century world that never existed before. A single bully can intimidate not only a single student but an entire classroom, an entire school, and even an entire community. The problem is underscored by research from the National School Safety Center and the United States Secret Service that indicates that bullying was involved in 80 percent of school shootings over the past two decades. The title in this series that addresses this problem is a valuable and essential tool for promoting safety and stopping bullying.

Another problem that has been highlighted by the media is the threat of violence on our school campuses. In reality, research tells us that schools are the safest place for young people to be. After an incident like Columbine or Sandy Hook, however, it is difficult for the public, including students, to understand that a youngster is a hundred times more likely to be assaulted or killed at home or in the community than at school. Students cannot help but absorb the fears that are so prevalent in our society. Therefore, a frank, realistic, discussion of this topic, one that avoids hysteria and exaggeration, is essential for our young people. This series offers a title on this topic that does exactly that. It addresses questions such as: How do you deal with a gunman on the campus? Should you run, hide, or confront? We do not want to scare our children; instead, we want to empower them and reassure them as we prepare them for such a crisis. The book also covers the changing laws and school policies that are being put in place to ensure that students are even safer from the threat of violence in the school.

"Stranger danger" is another safety threat that receives a great deal of attention in the modern world. Again, the goal should be to empower rather than terrify our children. The book in this series focusing on this topic provides young readers with the essential information that will help them be "safety smart," not only at school but also between home and school, at play, and even when they are home alone.

Alcohol and drug abuse is another danger that looms over our young people. As many as 10 percent of American high school students are alcoholics. Meanwhile, when one student was asked, "Is there a drug problem in your school?" her reply was, "No, I can get all the drugs I want." A book in this series focuses on this topic, giving young readers the information they need to truly comprehend that drugs and alcohol are major threats to their safety and well-being.

From peer pressure to natural disasters, from road dangers to sports safety, the Safety First series covers a wide range of other modern concerns. Keeping children and our schools safe is not an isolated challenge. It will require all of us working together to create a climate where young people can have safe access to the educational opportunities that will promote the success of all children as they transition into becoming responsible citizens. This series is an essential tool for classrooms, libraries, guidance counselors, and community centers as they face this challenge.

Dr. Ronald Stephens
Executive Director
National School Safety Center
www.schoolsafety.us

Words to Know

civilians: Ordinary people who are not members of the military or police.
finance: Having to do with money and banking.
resilient: Able to bounce back to normal.
extremists: People who are willing to take huge measures to achieve their goals.

Chapter One

Real-Life Stories

For Zoe Davis-Chanin, the morning of September 11, 2001, seemed just like any other morning. Her family lived in a small apartment near the financial district in Manhattan. She was woken up by her father, ate some breakfast, and got ready for school. She left the apartment, like she did every morning, and walked with her younger sister, Mara, to school. "I knew something was wrong because, on my way up to my 4th grade classroom, some friends of mine and I heard the principal scream in her office. We didn't think anything of it until we reached our classroom. There, we saw a burning hole in the side of one of the World Trade Center buildings. We all crowded around the windows to watch. It is a vision that I will never forget." Zoe was witnessing the beginning of the worst terrorist attack the United States has ever experienced.

THE TERRORIST ATTACKS ON 9/11

On the morning of September 11, 2001, four planes were taken over by a group of Muslim terrorists from the countries of Saudi Arabia, Egypt, Lebanon, and the United Arab Emirates. These terrorists had only one goal. They wanted to fly the planes into some very important American buildings. They wanted to use these planes as weapons to kill as many people as possible.

Two of the planes were flown into the two tallest towers of the World Trade Center. Called the

The events of September 11, 2001 were some of the most tragic in American history. This memorial in Washington, D.C., commemorates the lives of those lost in the Pentagon on that day.

Terrorism & Perceived Terrorism Threats

Twin Towers, these large buildings were used mostly for international *finance* and trading. They were the heart of New York City's financial district, located in Manhattan. The Twin Towers and five other buildings that made up the World Trade Center eventually fell as a result of the plane crashes.

Terrorists crashed the third plane into the Pentagon. The Pentagon is a large, five-sided office building located in Arlington County, Virginia. It is the headquarters of the U.S. Department of Defense and a symbol of the strength of America's military. The fourth plane crashed into a field near the Diamond T. Mine in Stonycreek Township, Pennsylvania. It is believed the terrorists who took over this plane planned on crashing it into the U.S. Capitol. The Senate and the House of Representatives, which together make up the legislative branch of the U.S. government, are housed in the Capitol. The plane never made it there, however, because of the bravery of a few passengers on the plane who fought the terrorists on board. Their bravery prevented many deaths and the possible destruction of the Capitol, a very important symbol of the American government.

In total, almost three thousand people died in the attacks. This includes the 227 *civilians* and 19 hijackers aboard the four planes. It was the deadliest attack ever seen on U.S. soil. And it made Americans all too aware of the dangers of terrorism.

ZOE REMEMBERS 9/11

"By the time that the second plane hit [the Twin Towers]," Zoe says, "all of the students in my school had been taken down to our gymnasium. Many of us had seen what happened but we weren't told anything and weren't allowed to talk to each other. We were told that our parents were on their way to pick us up."

Luckily, Zoe and Mara's father worked nearby and came, with their mother, to pick up the girls. They took Zoe and Mara outside to watch the awful events of that day. "Before the attacks," Zoe says, "I remember how permanent all of the buildings felt around me. My family and I had lived only a few blocks from the Twin Towers almost since I was born. They were part of my first memories. None of us could believe what we were watching."

According to Zoe, she and her family watched the towers until she witnessed something horrible. "I remember seeing small dots falling from the highest windows of the towers. I asked my dad what they were and he didn't answer. Much later, my dad told me that the little dots were people jumping out of the windows of the towers." About two hundred people lost their lives on 9/11 by jumping out of the windows of the World Trade Center. Most of these people were trapped on the upper floors of the skyscrapers. They either fell while searching for safety or jumped to escape the fire and smoke.

"We were still very close to the World Trade Center when the first tower fell," Zoe says. "A cloud of dust came toward us and everyone in the street turned to run. My dad grabbed me and Mara and dragged us away. It was the scariest moment of the whole experience. It is very frightening feeling so close to something so horrible."

Zoe and her family ran uptown. There they ran into some friends of Zoe's mother. "We knew these people well," Zoe says. "They looked confused and afraid. Everyone seemed confused that day. People were rushing back and forth as if they didn't know what to do or where was safe."

Soho, where Zoe's grandfather lived, is only about a mile from the World Trade Center. For those living so close to Ground Zero (what the site of the attack was called after the buildings were destroyed), 9/11 was truly devastating.

Terrorism & Perceived Terrorism Threats

The attack on September 11 had a lasting effect on New York City and the entire country. This memorial in Manhattan is at the site of the attack on the World Trade Center.

Zoe's mother invited her friends to go with them to Zoe's grandfather's apartment, located in a neighborhood known as Soho. Unfortunately, Zoe's grandfather wasn't home. The family spent some time trying to break into the apartment before one of his neighbors heard them in the hallway and let them into her apartment. "People were extremely kind to each other that day," Zoe says. "And even though everyone was afraid, most people reacted with kindness and bravery."

"We continued to follow 9/11 on the television while we were in the apartment of my grandfather's neighbor," Zoe says. "It was really strange, seeing them in person and then seeing them on the television. None of it seemed real."

Over four hundred police officers and firefighters gave their lives trying to save people from the Twin Towers. It was the most deadly event for firefighters in our nation's history. But the bravery of these men and women will never be forgotten.

Eventually, Zoe and her family were picked up and brought further uptown by one of Zoe's

After the attack on 9/11, many people were scared and afraid, and looked for someone to blame. Some people incorrectly thought that all Muslims hated Americans, and were responsible for the attack. Mosques like this were often the targets of vandalism.

14

Terrorism & Perceived Terrorism Threats

The Islamic Religion

Muslim people follow the religion of Islam. The Islamic religion is the second-largest religion in the world, with 1.6 billion followers worldwide. Muslim people believe there is only one God and that his word is written in their holy book, the Qur'an. They follow the teachings and example of Muhammad, considered by them to be the last prophet of God. Though the terrorists on 9/11 carried out their attacks in the name of the Islamic religion, most Muslims are very peaceful people. Only a very small number of Muslims would consider hurting an innocent person. These people are called "extremists," and it is important to remember there are extremists in almost every religion.

cousins. He brought them to the home of Zoe's aunt, where the family lived for the next three weeks. "There was too much dust in and around our apartment," Zoe says. "So we couldn't actually go home until the end of December, right before Christmas." After the three weeks at her aunt's house, the Federal Emergency Management Agency (FEMA) and the Red Cross paid for a hotel room for Zoe and her family to stay in.

"It was hard," Zoe said. "Four people and two dogs in a one-bed hotel room can be pretty cramped. For us, 9/11 wasn't just one awful day. It affected us for a few months." On November 22, 2001, just a few days before Thanksgiving, Zoe's family gave an interview on CNN, representing the many families who had to leave their homes following the awful terrorist attacks on 9/11. Zoe already mentioned how many people faced the tragedy on 9/11 with amazing acts of kindness and bravery. But on CNN, Zoe's mom showed how *resilient* the people of America can be by saying, "We are very thankful on this holiday to the whole country and for being alive. Because we were there that day and we, we're happy."

UNDERSTANDING 9/11

September 11, 2011, was a scary day for Zoe. It was a scary day for people all around the country. Zoe's story shows us what a terrorist attack is like through the eyes of one of the innocent people targeted by the attack. But Zoe learned many years later that "9/11 is a very complicated issue." According to Zoe, terrorism today happens for many reasons. And understanding the events that led to 9/11 can teach us an important lesson about why tragedies like this happen. And it can help us understand why terrorism is still a danger.

The story of September 11, 2001, began in 1991, when the country of Iraq invaded a small neighboring country called Kuwait. The invasion of Kuwait led to what we now call the Gulf War. In the Gulf War, the United States led troops from thirty-four countries to force the Iraqi military out of Kuwait. One of these countries was Saudi Arabia, which allowed the United States to set up military bases there in order to fight Iraq. But after the Gulf War, the United States stayed in Saudi Arabia so that they could keep a close watch over Iraq. The United States continued to keep troops in Saudi Arabia until 2003.

While most Muslims, including the government of Saudi Arabia, did not mind letting the U.S.

The war in Afghanistan was still being fought in 2014. It is likely that the country will bear the scars of this war for many years.

Terrorism & Perceived Terrorism Threats

military stay in Saudi Arabia, some Islamic **extremists** did not like the idea of letting the United States stay. Saudi Arabia is the home of two of the most holy places of the Islamic people. And Islamic extremists saw it as a crime that non-Muslims were allowed to stay there. As a result, Osama bin Laden, the leader of a group of Islamic extremists known as al-Qaeda, began a religious war against the United States. They saw forcing the United States out of Saudi Arabia as something worth killing innocent people over. Al-Qaeda claimed to be responsible for carrying out the tragedies on September 11, as well as many other terrorist attacks before and since.

In 1993, al-Qaeda carried out the first terrorist attack that targeted the World Trade Center. They set off a bomb below one of the Twin Towers that was meant to destroy both buildings. Though neither building was destroyed, six people died and over one thousand people were injured. And between 1993 and 2001, four more terrorist attacks were carried out by al-Qaeda against American people and troops in other countries. While many people were killed and nearly one thousand people were wounded, none of these terrorist attacks was nearly as large as those on 9/11.

After 9/11, the United States saw Afghanistan, the home of al-Qaeda, as one of the largest supporters of terrorism around the world. America began the War on Terror, in order to protect America. Less than a month after 9/11, the United States invaded Afghanistan to overthrow the Taliban, a group of Islamic extremists who supported al-Qaeda and controlled most of the country.

As of 2014, the War on Terror continued. Over two thousand U.S. soldiers and nearly fifteen thousand innocent civilians have died in the Afghanistan War. And extremists continue to plan terrorist attacks. They have attempted to attack the innocent civilians of the United States and Great Britain at least nine times since 2001.

But al-Qaeda isn't the only group carrying out terrorist attacks. And religious beliefs aren't the only reasons people carry out terrorist attacks. Some are carried out for political reasons or because the terrorist is mentally ill. It can be hard to tell exactly who a terrorist might be or what one might look like. And this is only part of the reason terrorism is so dangerous.

Words to Know

traumatic: Upsetting for a long time.
potential: Having to do with something that might happen.

Chapter Two

What Makes Terrorism Dangerous?

"As we all know from the aftermath of September 11, 2001, when we get scared enough, we are willing to do almost anything to [feel like] we are safe—even if this means giving up things we love," says Dr. Charles Raison in an article he wrote for CNN after the Boston Marathon bombings. The Boston Marathon bombings took place in 2013. Two bombs exploded during the Boston Marathon, killing three people and injuring 264. This is one example of how dangerous terrorism continues to be. But Dr. Raison, a mental health expert, understands that even though terrorism is dangerous, living in fear is the most dangerous effect terrorism can have.

TERRORISTS MAKES PEOPLE AND GOVERNMENTS AFRAID

Franklin D. Roosevelt, the thirty-second president, once said, "The only thing we have to fear is fear itself." President Roosevelt said this during the depths of the Great Depression, the worst period of economic collapse in America's history. Terrorism is very different than an economic collapse. Terrorism is any act of violence that is meant to inspire fear in a person or group of people, so Roosevelt's quote may be even more important to remember today.

19

Sometimes feeling the fight-or-flight response can be healthy or fun—like when you're paragliding—but if you feel it all the time or can't control your feelings of fear, it can hurt your quality of life.

Terrorism & Perceived Terrorism Threats

Terrorism Isn't New

Terrorism is often thought to be something new. But people have been using violence for religious or political reasons for a long time. Some scholars trace the use of violence for these means back to the first century. But the word "terrorism" first arose during the Reign of Terror. This was a period during the French Revolution, when France's ruling party publicly killed forty thousand people in order to make people obey the government. The word was used to refer to the French massacres until the mid-1800s. Anarchists (people who believe there should be no laws) and other political groups then began using terrorism to encourage revolution. Terrorism has also been used to support some causes that we would consider good today, such as ending slavery. Remember that no matter what the cause, if people are willing to hurt others to further the cause, they are extremists.

Our bodies naturally react when we are afraid. Your heart might beat faster when watching a scary movie. Or your palms might sweat when your teacher announces a pop quiz on a day that you forgot to do your homework. The body's reaction to fear is called the fight-or-flight response. And these reactions have been keeping people safe for a very long time.

Here's how it works. Imagine you live in the wilderness and have just come face-to-face with a dangerous animal. You have two choices if you don't want to be killed. You could run for it. Or you could pick up a stick or some other weapon and try to fight it. These are the fight-or-flight reactions.

To prepare for fight or flight, our bodies do a number of things automatically so they're ready for quick action or a quick escape. Our heart rate increases to pump more blood to our muscles and brains. We breathe faster to supply our bodies with oxygen. The pupils in our eyes get larger so that we can see better. And our digestive and urinary systems slow down for the moment, so we can concentrate on more important things.

All these reactions put our bodies and minds under a lot of stress. This stress is important for keeping us safe when we are in danger from something like a dangerous animal. This is called an immediate danger. But terrorist attacks do not happen every day. In fact, terrorist attacks are very rare. Sometimes we feel the fight-or-flight response even when we are not in immediate danger. This is called anxiety.

At least ten thousand firefighters, police officers, and civilians exposed to the terrorist attack on the World Trade Center have been found to have post-traumatic stress disorder (PTSD). PTSD is a mental illness where our flight-or-fight response refuses to shut itself off after a *traumatic* event.

We do not always think clearly when we are afraid. Have you ever said or done something foolish when you were afraid? This is because your body and mind were under stress and only wanted to keep you safe. According to Dr. Raison, we need to be careful about terrorist attacks. But, "We should not immediately change how we live our lives based on these [fearful] reactions."

Spending time being cautious and preparing for *potential* attacks are important in fighting

Americans are much more likely to die from familiar dangers like the health effects of cigarettes—but people often forget these dangers when they're worrying about terrorist attacks, which are much more unlikely.

Terrorism & Perceived Terrorism Threats

terrorism. But the people with PTSD show us that terrorism can trick our bodies into thinking we are in immediate danger even when we are not. This can cause us to spend too much time, effort, and money protecting ourselves from terrorism and not enough time worrying about those things that put us in danger every day.

TERRORISM MAKES US LOSE SIGHT OF OTHER DANGERS

Terrorism is meant to make us afraid or anxious. "Our brains and bodies are wired to be overly sensitive to threats," says Dr. Raison. Dr. Raison is talking about the fight-or-flight response. It helped keep us safe when we lived in the wilderness. Now it helps us when we face danger. Our brains think, *It is better to be awakened ten times in the middle of the night by a false alarm than to sleep blissfully just once while your house burns down around you.*

Not all threats make us afraid. The things that make us the most afraid are those that have threatened us the most over the millions of years that we have been evolving. But today, we do not need to be afraid of the same things that we used to be afraid of. "Consider, for example, that [before] the 19th century, no human traveled faster than the speed a horse can gallop," says Dr. Raison. "This explains why most of us fear flying far more than driving, even though driving is far more dangerous.

"Fearing heights promoted [our] survival over millions of years," Dr. Raison continues, but fearing driving something that traveled as fast as a car wouldn't have helped at all. This may be why so many people drive over the speed limit while driving a car—but why so many people are afraid to set foot on an airplane.

According to Dr. Raison, "[Terrorists] don't spend their efforts convincing us to drive faster, smoke cigarettes, or eat more processed food, which are the real killers in the modern world." Terrorists can make us lose sight of those things that put us in the most danger every day. And compared to terrorism, many of the threats that we experience—threats like unhealthy food, disease, poor education, and drugs—seem less immediate. The problem is these other dangers become all the more dangerous if we do not give them the time, money, and attention they deserve.

Even though terrorism might activate our flight-or-fight response, Dr. Raison believes the proper response to terrorists isn't necessarily increasing security or fearing public events. Instead, he says, we should try not to forget what today's dangers really are.

TERRORISTS WILL DO ANYTHING TO BE SEEN AND HEARD

While fear is perhaps the biggest danger that terrorism can have, one thing makes terrorists especially dangerous. Terrorists will stop at nothing and use any means necessary to have their message seen and heard.

Terrorism is any act meant to create fear or anxiety in a group of people. An act of terrorism can also be considered any attack carried out for religious or political reasons, or any attack that targets or disregards the safety of innocent people. When a person or group decides their religious or political views make it OK to kill innocent people, they have become extremists.

Extremists may kill others to protest a war. In 2009, for example, American soldier Nidal Malik

Post-traumatic stress disorder (PTSD) is a common problem among both soldiers and the victims of terrorism. By seeking to understand PTSD, mental health professionals are hoping to learn to better help those suffering from the negative effects of terrorism.

Terrorism & Perceived Terrorism Threats

Hasan began shooting his fellow soldiers in a military base in Fort Hood, Texas. Hasan was a military psychiatrist. He mostly worked with soldiers suffering from PTSD. While it is hard to determine exactly what caused Hasan to shoot others, his family told reporters that he turned against the Iraq and Afghanistan wars after hearing stories soldiers told him about serving there.

Since the attack, Hasan has claimed to be an Islamic extremist. He has said he feels that the American wars on Iraq and Afghanistan were wars against Islam. He felt he could no longer defend a country fighting a war against his people.

Terrorism happens for lots of reasons. But we don't need to let fear of terrorism control our lives!

SEVERE
SEVERE RISK OF TERRORIST ATTACKS

HIGH
HIGH RISK OF TERRORIST ATTACKS

ELEVATED
SIGNIFICANT RISK OF TERRORIST ATTACKS

GUARDED
GENERAL RISK OF TERRORIST ATTACKS

LOW
LOW RISK OF TERRORIST ATTACKS

Words to Know

intelligence: The information spies gather from other countries.
public-sector: Having to do with businesses and services carried out by the government.
monitor: Watch, keep track of.

Chapter Three

Staying Safe and Being Prepared

"Terrorism is a global issue," says Nathan Feldman, "so it takes a lot more than a few people and few precautions to keep us safe." Nathan has worked in counterterrorism for a number of years. An important part of his job is gathering information on suspected terrorists. But as Nathan says, "It takes a strong community and strong country to stay safe from terrorism."

PREVENTING TERRORISM: GOVERNMENTAL AGENCIES

According to Nathan, having strong civilian organizations, such as the Red Cross, is an important part of being ready for a terrorist attack. "But these organizations," Nathan says, "can only prepare us for effectively handling a terrorist attack once it's happened. They can do very little to prevent a terrorist attack."

Part of what makes terrorism so hard to combat is that it is an international issue. "If I want to go to another country," Nathan says, "I have to have a passport so that both America and the country that I am going to know who I am, where I am, and how long I plan on staying." As Nathan has pointed out, governments oversee international travel. This is part of how governments deal with international relations. Imagine two countries as two neighboring houses. If you wanted to go into your neighbor's house to change something, you would need to ask his or her

New laws passed after 9/11 allowed government organizations like the NSA to start monitoring peoples' communications in the name of preventing terrorism. This resulted in controversy about whether people had a right to privacy or not.

Terrorism & Perceived Terrorism Threats

permission first. The government needs to ask permission to enter another country in order to fight terrorism.

Many government agencies help fight terrorism. They include the Department of Homeland Security (DHS), Federal Bureau of Investigation (FBI), the National Security Agency (NSA), the Transportation Safety Agency (TSA), and the Central Intelligence Agency (CIA). These agencies work around the clock to prevent the terrorist attacks that are being planned on the people of America. "Sometimes, it seems like we have so many governmental agencies," Nathan says. "I imagine that it would be hard for a civilian to keep track of everything that they do to protect us."

Our government has many ways to keep us safe. And not all Americans agree on how our government keeps us safe. Part of the problem is that in order to effectively fight terrorism, the government keeps some of these programs a secret. But there is information available about most of the government agencies working to stop terrorism.

The National Joint Terrorism Task Force, for example, is just one of the many antiterrorism programs led by these agencies. Run by the FBI, the National Joint Terrorism Task Force manages all the Joint Terrorism Task Forces (JTTFs) located around the country. The JTTF is a network of investigators from dozens of U.S. law enforcement and intelligence agencies. Today, there are over one hundred JTTFs located in almost every one of America's major cities.

The National Joint Terrorism Task Force oversees the more than four thousand members of the individual JTTFs. Making sure everyone has the information and resources they need can be a very hard job. But the National Joint Terrorism Task Force helps them share important information and provides them with the guidance, training, and resources needed to be successful. According to the FBI, "When it comes to investigating terrorism, [JTTFs] do it all: chase down leads, gather evidence, make arrests, provide security for special events, conduct training, collect and share *intelligence*, and respond to threats and incidents at a moment's notice."

Since the terrorist attacks of 9/11, over seventy new JTTFs were formed. They have already been important in the fight against terrorism. They have stopped a number of large-scale terrorist attacks on the United States. And they've even traced sources of terrorist funding, responded to the threat of chemical weapons, halted the use of fake IDs, and quickly arrested suspicious characters with many kinds of deadly weapons and explosives.

The DHS is also actively involved in the fight to prevent terrorism. This agency was started after 9/11 in order to help strengthen America's defenses against terrorist plans. Its Nationwide Suspicious Activity Reporting Initiative, for example, teaches our law enforcers how to identify and report suspicious activity that may be related to terrorist activities. To date, nearly 230,000 law enforcers have received Suspicious Activity Reporting training thanks to the DHS.

The DHS also heads the National Terrorism Advisory System. In the case of a terrorist threat, this system sends out alerts to the public, government agencies, disaster relief coordinators, *public-sector* organizations, and transportation centers, like airports.

Programs like the National Joint Terrorism Task Force and the National Terrorism Advisory System show us how important information is in the fight against terrorism. "Information" is really just a fancy word for any kind of message. A message, in this case, can be anything as simple

When George W. Bush announced the beginning of the War of Terror, the decision sparked controversy all over the nation. More than a decade later, the war was still underway—and there was more disagreement than ever.

Terrorism & Perceived Terrorism Threats

Not everyone agrees that military action is the best way to fight terrorism. It's a complicated issue that has divided the American people since the war started in 2001.

as visiting an extremist website or contacting known extremist groups. Many government agencies **monitor** the communications between suspected terrorists in order to stop any plans that they might have. Information may just be the best way we have to prevent further terrorist attacks.

THE MILITARY AND THE WAR ON TERROR

After the World Trade Center attacks on 9/11, the American government responded by beginning the War on Terror. The War on Terror refers to the actions that our military and other government agencies have taken to protect Americans and to wipe out terrorism once and for all.

When President George W. Bush, announced the War on Terror, he said the United States had five main goals:

- Defeat terrorists, such as Osama bin Laden, and demolish their organizations.
- Identify, locate, and demolish terrorists and their organizations.

In 2001, the government of Afghanistan was known to be corrupt. One of the justifications for the war was to drive out terrorists and put a strong government in place in Afghanistan.

Terrorism & Perceived Terrorism Threats

Controversial Tactics: Surveillance

Our government agencies work hard to prevent terrorist attacks. They have already stopped many attacks, not only in America, but also around the world. But some of the tactics that these agencies use are very controversial. When something is controversial, not everyone agrees on it. The TSA, for example, has been criticized many times for stereotyping Muslims and making them go through unfair safety procedures based on their religious practices or appearance. The NSA faced criticism in 2013, after Edward Snowden, who was employed by a company working for the agency, released documents that showed the agency had been collecting data on the e-mail and phone records of millions of Americans.

- Deny terrorists' support and places to hide.
- Help prevent conditions that can lead to terrorism.
- Defend U.S. citizens and interests at home and abroad.

The first two goals may seem similar, but they are both important. The first goal suggests that our military is chasing down terrorists we already knew were a threat to America when the president set out the goals. So far, this first goal has been successful. In 2011, a few months before the tenth anniversary of September 11, our military killed Osama bin Laden in a raid in the country of Pakistan.

The second goal, on the other hand, shows we are also dedicated to uncovering new threats against America—before these terrorists attack. This involves not only chasing down terrorist groups but also monitoring information to see if any potential terrorist threats can be spotted ahead of time.

The third goal is a complicated one and involves not only our military but representatives of the United States. This goal involves ending the practice of governments supporting terrorist groups. For the United States, supporting a terrorist group is when a government gives them money, weapons, or places to hide. As already mentioned, international relations can be tough. And using force is often not the answer. In these situations, the U.S. government may send elected officials and diplomats to reason with those governments to get them on our side.

The fourth goal is also complicated. It involves strengthening so-called weak states. A weak state is any country with a weak government or a weak economic system. A good example is Afghanistan before the War on Terror began. Before America invaded Afghanistan in 2001, the country was governed by a group of Islamic extremists known as the Taliban. While the Taliban was in power, they enforced a very strict version of Islamic law. They also supported Osama bin Laden and al-Qaeda. The U.S. invasion of Afghanistan was designed to overthrow the Taliban. But it was also designed to replace the Taliban government with a strong democracy, which would be more like the U.S. government. It would also help grow Afghanistan's economy.

The War on Terror has seen the rise of a new kind of warfare, fought with unmanned drones instead of risking the lives of soldiers as often.

34

Terrorism & Perceived Terrorism Threats

The fifth and final goal shows us that the War on Terror isn't only about fighting terrorism. It is also about keeping Americans safe from terrorists. But as Nathan says, "The War on Terror has been controversial for many years now." Some people think the presence of our military in other countries has turned some people into extremists. Other people think our wars in Afghanistan and Iraq have made these countries less stable, and this could lead to even more terrorist attacks.

The war in Iraq has ended, and the war in Afghanistan was set to end in 2014. But most people do not realize the War on Terror involves a lot more than only these two wars. It is likely to continue for a long time to come.

Words to Know

evacuate: Leave for safety reasons.
vigilant: On guard against danger, paying attention.

Chapter Four

What Can You Do to Stay Safe?

"It may seem like terrorism is something that young people couldn't do much about," says Joanna Schneider. Joanna has been working in disaster preparation and relief for many years. Her job is to prepare for disasters and to act quickly when they strike. An act of terrorism affects a lot of people. This means it takes an entire community of alert and prepared people to defend against terrorism. "This includes our young people," Joanna says.

BE PREPARED, AND KNOW WHAT TO DO

Organizations like FEMA and the Red Cross are organized to be able to respond to disasters, like terrorist attacks, anywhere in the country. But Joanna says, "Families and communities also need to organize so that they can respond quickly and effectively to any disaster."

Young people should know if their communities or schools have emergency plans for disasters, like terrorist attacks. Some schools and communities are located in places where a terrorist attack is unlikely. Terrorists tend to attack highly populated areas, such as cities, in order to make as much damage as possible. Many of these schools and communities do not bother to make

If you and your family have a plan for what to do in an emergency, then you don't have to worry as much about whether one will happen—if it does, you'll be ready!

Terrorism & Perceived Terrorism Threats

If a terrorist attack ever happened, people will be afraid and lines of communication might be down or overloaded. Arranging a place to meet your family ahead of time—like the mall—is important in case you're unable to contact each other.

emergency plans. But if your school or community has an emergency plan, you should know what it is and how to follow it.

"Emergency plans are especially important for families," Joanna says. Ask your parents if they have an emergency contact set up in case of a disaster or terrorist attack. An emergency contact is someone your family knows who lives far enough away that they probably wouldn't be affected by the same event. "Emergency contacts will be able to check on each other if a disaster occurs," Joanna says. "If I was your emergency contact and I couldn't get in contact with you during a disaster, I would be able to call the police and let them know that you are missing." This may seem like a simple step, but in the case of a disaster, getting an injured person help quickly can be the difference between living and dying.

What Can You Do to Stay Safe?

In an emergency, people like police officers and firefighters are there to help you. If you can, make sure you help others, too—the best way to get through a difficult situation is to work together!

Terrorism & Perceived Terrorism Threats

"Families should also have a meeting place that they all know about," Joanna says. Terrorist attacks happen quickly, and you might need to *evacuate* your home or school without waiting for your parents. If this happens, knowing your parents will meet you at a specific location can be a great way to avoid unnecessary fear and confusion.

"Another situation," Joanna says, "is that you are not allowed to leave your home for a long time." A terrorist attack may make it too dangerous to travel. In this case, you will need to have certain supplies in your home in order to survive. Keep such things as first-aid supplies, a battery-powered radio or television, extra batteries, food, bottled water, and tools on hand for emergencies. "And preparing a bag of essentials for having to evacuate is a good idea too," Joanna says. "You should have certain items in an easy-to-carry bag at all times." According to Joanna, these items include a change of clothing for each member of your family, a sleeping bag for each, some cash, and copies of important family documents (birth certificates, passports, and licenses).

These important steps will help keep you safe not only from terrorism but from most kinds of disasters. But being prepared is only half the battle. It is also important to know what to do if you ever find yourself near a terrorist attack. The Red Cross lists the following guidelines for anyone caught in a terrorist attack:

- Remain calm and be patient.
- Follow the advice of local emergency officials.
- Listen to your radio or television for news and instructions.
- If the event occurs near you, check for injuries.
- Give first aid and get help for seriously injured people.
- If the event occurs near your home while you are there, check for damage using a flashlight. Do not light matches or candles or turn on electrical switches. Check for fires, fire hazards, and other household hazards. Sniff for gas leaks, starting at the water heater. If you smell gas or suspect a leak, turn off the main gas valve, open windows, and get everyone outside quickly.
- Shut off any other damaged utilities.
- Make sure your pets are safe and can't run away.
- Call your family contact—do not use the telephone again unless it is a life-threatening emergency.
- Check on your neighbors, especially those who are elderly or disabled.

IF YOU SEE SOMETHING, SAY SOMETHING

"Being able to respond quickly and effectively to a disaster is important," Joanna says. "But terrorism is a unique kind of disaster. Earthquakes or tornadoes, for example, are hard to predict and often take us by surprise. But terrorist attacks can be prevented."

Terrorist attacks, like those on 9/11, most often take us by surprise. Our military and government agencies are working hard to prevent terrorists from surprising us anymore. But what Joanna

When the car bomb was discovered in Times Square, many of the buildings and theaters nearby were evacuated while the authorities dealt with the bomb. By working together, everyone managed to prevent a disaster!

Terrorism & Perceived Terrorism Threats

Become Informed About Your Government and Other Cultures

Nothing our government could ever do would make it OK to kill innocent people. But most people do not understand why a terrorist would hate us. They might think it is because a terrorist is "crazy" or "evil." Some terrorists are mentally ill, but these terrorists usually work alone. Some people have this view of terrorists, because they do not fully understand what our government is doing overseas. If they are aware of our government's actions, they may not care how these actions impact other cultures. Become informed about your government and the other cultures our government deals with. If you see something you do not like, say something. Inform other people about it. The right to do this is what makes America special. And exercising this right is one of the best ways to show the terrorists that we will not be beaten.

means is that it is not only our government's responsibility to keep ourselves and others safe from terrorist attacks. It is our responsibility, too.

The DHS recently launched a campaign to inform people about this responsibility. Their motto is simple: If you see something, say something. In other words, if you see suspicious activity, you should tell a parent or call the police.

But it is important to understand what exactly they mean by suspicious activity. This does not mean being afraid and calling the police just because you see someone of a different race, ethnicity, national origin, or religious affiliation. Terrorists can come in all shapes and sizes, and focusing on someone's outsides can distract us from the real dangers around us. Instead, the DHS suggests reporting behaviors and situations like an unattended backpack in a public place or seeing someone trying to trespass.

A terrorist tried to set off a car bomb in Times Square in New York City in 2010. He did not make his bomb correctly, which prevented it from being too dangerous. But even if it was, the bomb may not have been successful. Why? Because a street vendor noticed smoke coming from the car and flagged down a police officer. According to President Obama, the attack, "failed because ordinary citizens were *vigilant* and reported suspicious activities to authorities. It failed because authorities from the local, state, and federal acted quickly. And did what they planned to do."

BE PREPARED, NOT AFRAID

In chapter 2, Dr. Raison talked about how important it is to be cautious and prepared for a terrorist attack. But more important, he talked about how the point of terrorism is in the name: terrorism spreads terror. Spreading fear is one of the main goals of all terrorism. And being afraid and acting in fear lets terrorism win.

A FEMA staff member teaches a child about how to prepare for a disaster like terrorism. FEMA sponsors family events like this around the country, with a range of safety and preparedness activities, including practice 911 calls and home evacuation.

Terrorism & Perceived Terrorism Threats

"Being prepared," Joanna says, "may seem like something that people do when they are afraid. But being prepared can make us less afraid. It can give us assurance that if anything were to go wrong, that we had a plan would avoid unneeded harm." Like Dr. Raison, Joanna suggests being just cautious enough and then not worrying about it anymore. "Feeling unsafe in your own home can be one of the most fearful things that a person can face," she says. But refusing to be afraid and continuing to live a happy life is the best way to combat every form of terrorism.

Find Out More

ONLINE

History of Terrorism
hnn.us/articles/299.html

Terrorism
www.fbi.gov/about-us/investigate/terrorism

Terrorism
kidshealth.org/kid/feeling/thought/terrorist_attacks.html

Terrorism
www.nctsn.org/trauma-types/terrorism

Terrorism Prevention
www.redcross.org/prepare/disaster/terrorism

IN BOOKS

Nardo, Don. *The History of Terrorism*. North Mankato, Minn.: Compass Point Books, 2010.

Netzley, Patricia D. *Terrorism and War of the 2000s (The Decade of the 2000s)*. San Diego, Calif.: Referencepoint Press, 2013.

Sherrow, Victoria. *Homegrown Terror: The Oklahoma City Bombings*. Berkeley Heights, N.J.: Enslow Publishers, 2013.

Sterngass, Jon. *Terrorism (Debating the Issues)*. Tarrytown, N.Y.: Marshall Cavendish Children's Books, 2011.

Woolf, Alex. *Terrorism (Global Issues)*. New York: Rosen Central, 2011.

Index

About the Author & Consultant

Christie Marlowe was raised in New York City where she lives with her husband and works as a writer, journalist, and web designer.

Dr. Ronald D. Stephens currently serves as executive director of the National School Safety Center. His past experience includes service as a teacher, assistant superintendent, and school board member. Administrative experience includes serving as a chief school business officer, with responsibilities over school safety and security, and as vice president of Pepperdine University.

Dr. Stephens has conducted more than 1000 school security and safety site assessments throughout the United States. He was described by the *Denver Post* as "the nation's leading school crime prevention expert." Dr. Stephens serves as consultant and frequent speaker for school districts, law enforcement agencies and professional organizations worldwide. He is the author of numerous articles on school safety as well as the author of *School Safety: A Handbook for Violence Prevention*. His career is distinguished by military service. He is married and has three children.

Picture Credits